Whatsoever Things

Are Lovely . . .

Whatsoever Things Are Lovely . . .

HELEN SUTTON BOOTH

GARDEN CITY, NEW YORK

DOUBLEDAY & COMPANY, INC.

1972

Some of the poems in this volume were previously published in the following periodicals: "Advent," *The Diplomat*; "Flight," the New York *Times*, copyright © 1959 by Helen Sutton Booth; "Autumn Cadenza," reprinted by permission from *The Christian Science Monitor*, © 1967 The Christian Science Publishing Society, all rights reserved; "The Gardener," "First In Peace," the Washington *Evening Star*; "Strange Interlude," "Prayer For a Young Student," "The Mother," *Youth's Instructor*, copyright © 1964 by Review & Herald Publishing Association; "Jacob's Ladder," "The Lincoln Memorial," "November Topaz," *The Magnificat*.

To Kyle, Helen Elaine, and Virginia

CONTENTS

Part II: Seasons

Part IV: Think on These Things

Whatsoever Things
Are Lovely . . .

PART I

This Is the Day Which the Lord Hath Made

THIS IS THE DAY WHICH
THE LORD HATH MADE

At dawn I know the sun's bright edge
Will pierce the dimness and the mist
And slowly light the sleeping world
With lamps of gold and amethyst.
And I know that on barren hills
The trees' stark branches wait for spring,
That tides go out but to return
And answer follows questioning.

DAYBREAK

LET US REJOICE AND BE GLAD IN IT

At daybreak the Heavens declare the glory of God.
We sense His presence in the beauty of the dawn.
In quiet majesty the sun arises, the villages and cities
quiver with life.
Yesterday is a passing dream, lost in the maze of time.
We do not know what tomorrow may bring.
So let us rejoice and give thanks for this glad, new day.

LET US GIVE THANKS

Let us give thanks that we have rested
in peace and safety throughout the night,
For the comforting presence of our loved ones,
The dear, familiar sights and sounds of morning,
The glad voices of children,
A carillon of birds outside the window,
The awakening world about us and the renewed
strength for the tasks that lie ahead.

THESE ARE THE MOMENTS OF ETERNITY

This is the day of salvation when all things are made new.
We accept it, dear Lord, as Thy divine gift,
fresh and beautiful.
May we keep it unshadowed by the cares of yesterday
or dread of tomorrow,
Undefiled by bitterness, strife or ill-speaking
as we walk in Thy presence.
Temper our spirits and illume our minds that we
may know these are the moments of eternity.

NOW ABIDETH FAITH, HOPE AND LOVE,
BUT THE GREATEST OF THESE IS LOVE

The silver poplar always bends
To meet an untried breeze
With music like a singing harp
And upturned singing leaves.

Day lilies, dew filled, face the sun
Reflecting amber glow,
The waves will break on a tranquil sea
Whatever winds may blow.

So walking on unchartered paths
We turn our hearts to Thee
That we reflect a shining faith
And deep serenity.

LET US REJOICE IN FAITH

Light our darkened paths each hour
with a glowing faith,
Strengthen our faltering wills and faint hearts
with the certain knowledge of divine goodness.

Give us faith in ourselves, knowing
we are children of God, and faith in our fellow men
that all things work together for good for those
who love Thee.

LET US REJOICE IN HOPE

As the morning hours pass into noontide,
keep our hearts singing.
Sanctify our hopes and longings. May we
work with others in harmony and peace.
Reconcile our restless spirits and rebellious hearts
when we are frustrated and disappointed
in realizing our fondest dreams.
We would follow in the footsteps of those
who have walked in Thy light in confidence and quietness
that we shall do greater things.

THE GREATEST OF THESE IS LOVE

We thank Thee for love that has power and is sustaining,
That forgives all ills and keeps no score of wrongs,
That is enduring and reaches out towards all mankind.
Love that encompasses us as a shield, keeping
all hatred and suspicion from our hearts, reaching
far beyond our mortal span into eternity,
That keeps us above pettiness, tempering
our judgments and curbing our impatience.
Whatever comes this day, dear Lord, may love direct our
    paths.

GOD HAS SET THE SOLITARY IN FAMILIES

We pray that love may transform our relationships with
    others.
We rejoice in the wonder and innocence of childhood,
the dreams and hopes of youth, the achievements of maturity
and memories and contentment of those who have grown
    older.
Help us to give our best to those who are nearest and dearest
    to us,
that no petty differences or worldly ambitions can separate us.
Give us a genuine reverence for the personality of each,
remembering they are not ours but Thine.
May we love them as Thy children, each endowed
with unique gifts and infinite abilities.

AFTERNOON

THE TRUTH SHALL MAKE YOU FREE

Keep our minds open to new truth,
that we may grow in wisdom and grace.
As new wine must be put into new bottles, grant us
new revelations each day.
Give us courage to face new truths and charter new paths,
renouncing our stubborn wills and outworn traditions.
Let us put away our old selves with the certain knowledge
that God has made more Truth to come forth from His word.

7

WHATSOEVER THY HANDS FIND TO DO

Lord, if today my path shall lie
In ways of humble duty,
In obscure service let me find
New meaning and new beauty,
And murmur not against the care
That each new day comes bringing
But gild the dullness of each task
That I shall do it singing.

LET US REJOICE IN WORK

Grant us joy in creative labor, knowing
There is no virtue in work for its own sake
Remembering that without vision a people perish
And works without faith are dead,
Serving our fellow men with joy and relinquishing
Our futile plans and foolish ambitions to help them,
Forgive our prejudices and uncompromising attitudes
As we honestly strive to bring about Thy kingdom
On earth ever seeking to give all men a chance
At the best things in life.

THE LORD LOOKETH UPON THE HEART

May we not take too seriously the things that
seem to be against us, knowing that the Lord
looketh upon the heart.
Inspire us to use our ordinary abilities
to perform uncommon tasks, without complaining
or self pity.
Keep us in the presence of the best that we may grow
in stature doing Thy will, not judging our success
by outward symbols.
Give us understanding hearts that we are in harmony
with our fellow men and with Thee.

IN CONFIDENCE AND QUIETNESS

Let us rejoice that we may stand with Thee
on some Mount of Transfiguration and share
Thy holy vision. As we go into the valley of
service to work with Thy children, give us
compassion and love. May we be patient in
discouragement and never lose sight of Thy
purpose for us.
　　And if it be that we shall do
　　Such deeds as men shall praise,
　　If our fame should win renown
　　And honor crown our days,
　　In the hour of triumph, Lord,
　　Keep our feet from straying
　　Should we be worthy of men's praise
　　We would receive it praying.

GRANT HEALING AND REST

Evening approaches with healing and rest.
Refresh the laborer who has worked in the field,
shop or factory. Inspire the wearied teacher, writer
and ministers in Thy vineyard.
Give renewed strength to overburdened parents and weary
  children.
Touch the hearts of any who are cruel, unjust or unkind.
Let faith be a healing balm to the discouraged and cynical.
Grant travel mercy to all returning home from country lanes,
or crowded streets, and protection and skill to all who guide
our journeys on land, sea and air.
Wherever we are when darkness falls, give us healing and
  peace.

TWILIGHT

We rejoice when twilight comes and find our rest in Thee,
grateful we have been given strength for the day's work.
With all Thy creation, we await Transition's mystery.
Grant peace and contentment as shadows gather
and tender silence falls upon the clamorous voices of the day.
Transform our restless activity into peaceful reflection,
renew wearied spirits as dusk falls like a silken veil
over the distant hills.
We close our eyes knowing we have walked with Thee this
  day.

WHITE CATHEDRAL

A white cathedral stood in wintry wood
Whose dim, unlighted spires were spruce and pine
Each bush, a gleaming altar stood
With crystal goblets for communion wine.
Upon a cloth of lacy filigree
Were mounds of snow for sacramental bread,
There was no sound, no bird in bush or tree,
But in snow-cloistered aisles I bowed my head.

TESTAMENT

I can forget the drifted snow
To dream how soon again
Blue hyacinths that sleep below
Will thread the garden lane.

And I can hear in elm's stark bough
The echo of a song
Arising in the wind's deep sigh
When nights seem dark and long.

Whatever comes I shall not fear,
Though human ills are rife,
Some hidden beauty will appear,
There is no death, but life!

HIS GARDEN

I like to think the garden where He rose
From dreamless sleep when He was laid in myrrh
Is lovely still: there now the lily grows
And shadowed leaves of olive branches stir.
Perhaps there now small children are at play
With joy and wonder shining in their eyes
The women knew, who waited for the day
And with its dawning saw their Lord arise.

And I can sense the hope each year reborn
When violets spring from the common sod
Dispelling doubt as even Thomas knew
Who touched His wounds and knew that He was God.
I think His garden must be lovely still
Who died for us upon that cruel hill.

STRANGE DARKNESS

There were no stars to pierce the gloom
The rising wind grew chill
The hours He lay within the tomb
When all the world was still.
Small children feared the sudden dark
Befalling them at play
While sages looked for sign to mark
Swift ending of the day.

For none believed the night would end
Save those who watched alone,
But stirring in the shadowed grass,
The lily must have known.

EASTER MAGIC

No blade of grass appears
On shop-lined thoroughfare
Where snarling traffic weaves
The hawkers shout their ware,
But Easter magic shines
On a shabby, slanting sill
Where, bravely and alone
There blooms a daffodil.

COMMUNION

There is no need for bread and wine
Each new day is a sacrament.
Deep-red, there glows in eastern sky
A symbol of the love He spent.
White driftwood washed upon the shore,
The mirrored sun on tranquil sea
And His voice borne on homing tide:
"When this ye do, remember me."

THE ROSE

God wanted all the loveliness
Of every flower that blows
Close hidden in one little bud
And so He made the rose.
He touched her petals with the tints
That sweep the morning skies,
The golden and the crimson hues
That fade as daylight dies.

A symbol of His love for us
Whatever wind may blow
Its beauty is a healing balm
The troubled heart may know
A rosebush is no hapless plant
Of root and stalk and sod,
It breathes and glows in ecstasy,
The very song of God.

14

GARDEN LINEAGE

When crimson hollyhocks, grown straight and tall
flaunt their bright colors over garden wall,
low beds of pansies under dogwood tree
wear regal velvet with humility.

THE GARDENER

Dear Lord, be kind for she has come
To live in your not far-off home
After long, weary months of pain
And eager she will be again
For some accustomed, well-loved task
So this, for her dear sake we ask:

Let there be something she can do
With gardens like she loved and knew
While here. She went too soon
For garden's loveliness this June.
So let death's narrow gate unfold
A beauty here, undreamed, untold.
For palaces she will not care,
But let her find a garden there.

PRAYER FOR AN ARTIST

Since often she revealed to us
The loveliness of sky and sea,
The glory of the lifted hill,
And seasons in their majesty,
May beauty that is rarer far
Unfold before her wondering eyes
With friends that she has loved and known.
Make beautiful her Paradise.

AUTUMN (AFTER TSCHAIKOWSKY)

Who has not sensed in autumn's somber mood
a motif of Tschaikowsky symphony,
heard rising crescendo of violin
when bitter wind assails a giant tree,
or echo of the heart's deep questioning
as stalwart oak, her russet beauty gone
awaits alone first flute-like call of spring
as hearts bereft have done since time began?

SUNDAY MORNING

When all the sounds of gaiety are hushed
There comes the silence of approaching dawn,
White clouds appear in flowing priestly robes,
Their changing stoles red, lavender, and gold.
This solemn hour is neither day nor night,
Nor sleep nor waking, yet its moments hold
The echo of songs quivering in air,
And voice of prophets calling men to prayer.

New fallen oak leaves stir in yellowed grass,
Half-dreaming households stir, aroused by thud
Of morning paper tossed against the door
And chime of distant bells. As last star wanes,
Tall candles light dim altars of the sky,
The kneeling hills arise and day begins.

REMEMBERED AUTUMN

(Nüremberg, 1947)

There was an autumn, crimson, yellow, blue
That touched the ruins of a once-proud town
In mellow tones of ever-changing hue.
The linden trees with golden spears marched down
Dark canyoned streets, with rubble heaped nearby,
Where houses stood, their rafters gaunt and bare,
Were softly veiled beneath October sky
By smoke-blue haze drifting thinly in air.
The song of Meistersingers echoed still
Above the moat and ivied castle wall,
Carnations cried from every flaming sill
Till swirling leaves began at last to fall,
Covering earth with royal tapestries,
Restoring splendor and past majesty.

TRANSITION

All things await Transition's mystery:
A tender silence broods on lifted hill
Where autumn beauty lingers to fulfill
The promises of April's budding tree.
These are the moments of eternity,
A quiet loveliness remaining till
Sharp winter comes and brooks lie numb and still
To dream of violets. So it will be

When we have reached the fullness of our year
And sense at last the imminence of change
The falling leaf, the ember's dying light
Will not dismay, for these shall reappear
In realms beyond, and nothing will seem strange
As we approach the coming of long night.

BETHLEHEM

Out of the silence there rang a song
Out of the dimness gleamed a star
Wondering, shepherds left their flocks
Wise men followed from afar.

Into men's hearts came joy and peace
Into the sky a heavenly light,
A mother smiled upon her babe,
And Lo! the babe was Christ.

ADVENT

So small were we, we stood tip-toe
To watch the gently falling snow
Hang stars on fir trees, ice-spun canes,
Spread angel wings on fields and lanes.

Though high drifts kept the barn from sight,
We knew the Child would come that night
To bless for us on Christmas Day,
The gifts we placed beside the hay.

AT THE INN

Small children wakened from their sleep
when heavenly music filled the sky
heard echoing throughout the night
sweet strains of Mary's lullaby.

The footsore travelers who came
crowding the inn from near and far
forgot their weariness to look
with wonder on a shining star.

The keeper who denied Him room
went humbly to the near-by shed
and knelt before the sleeping Babe
while shepherds worshipped at His bed.

WINTER QUIESCENCE

Now is the time pale, fading light
And bleak days tell the end is near
When in the hush of a dreamless night
Bells will toll for a dying year.
A year that spun the warm, spring sod,
Ripe orchards, molten summer field,
Blue gentian and the golden rod
In tapestries of autumn yield.

This year will pass in timeless sleep,
Quiescent and remote from all
Desire to sow or need to reap,
Past seasons' sharp, insistent call
To die with secrets locked in streams
And frozen oceans, white and still,
While promise waits in ice-bound trees
And crocus dreams upon the hill.

THIS NEW YEAR

As somnolent as a sleeping child,
Indifferent to tolling bell
Or sum of all our yesterdays
The New Year dawns. Who dares foretell
What it may bring of good or ill
When the first feasting days are past
Speaks foolishly as men who watch
Their first-born sleeping through closed glass.

VALE

Hold lighted candles in your hand
Casting their radiance everywhere,
Familiar street and distant land
Men lost in darkness and despair.

Keep prayer ever in your heart
For higher goals as time goes by,
That richer wisdom you impart,
Light candles now and hold them high!

PART II

Seasons

WINTER SILHOUETTE

Etched against my window pane
the trees' dark forms are seen,
each slender, curving twig retouched
with lines of silver sheen.
Clear across the farthest bough
a magic web is spun
of opalescent tapestries
that sparkle in the sun.

It seems that only kings should walk
beneath such pageantry,
a fairy's bower night will crown
with jeweled canopy,
but even as glad shouts go up
no monarch goes below,
just children making zigzag paths
while playing in the snow.

THIS GLAD NEW YEAR

New Year, with chiming bells, the scent of fir and pine
and our loved ones beside us in the firelight.
A day of mirth and feasting, reflection and anticipation.
A time for honest appraisal of ourselves when we resolve
to do better.
May the God who guided all of our yesterdays in ways of
faith, hope and love, teach us to treasure each hour as
a fragment of eternity.
Our times are in Thy hand and the future known only to
Thee.
Make each dawn a sacrament, each noontide a prayer
and when evening falls, give us Thy heavenly benediction.

STRANGE INTERLUDE

So closely are we bound to earth
by miracle of falling snow
our lives become safe, homeward paths
and comfort of the fireside's glow.

Once lost in too-familiar scenes
wild dreams are lost in things that are,
a drifted field our universe,
a snowflake greater than a star.

FEBRUARY

February! A short month with cold days and burning
sunsets. A fairy land of icy filigree without and warmth
and comfort within, drifts of snow on the window ledge
and the elm's dark branches etched against the pane.
We celebrate the birthdays of Washington and Lincoln
with speeches and waving flags. Crowds visit Mount Vernon
and the Lincoln Memorial. We remember Valley Forge
and Gettysburg.
Saint Valentine's Day comes with red hearts, bright candles
and elusive dreams of love.
Lord, we thank Thee for these special days and the radiance
they bring. And we thank Thee too that the first snowdrops
are in bloom under the elm.

FIRST IN PEACE

The river flows so quietly today
as on his tomb the glossy wreaths are lain
and reverently the crowds go on their way
to the home he loved through years of war and pain.
They pause beneath the holly tree and yew
and in his garden sense the peace he knew
still lingering in fragrant boxwood rows
and mignonette, soft veiled by melting snows.

GEORGE WASHINGTON'S CHURCH

In old Christ Church tall candles softly glow
on the altar where he knelt so long ago.
Great men now worship in his famous pew
and humble pray as he was wont to do.

For his birthday a shining wreath is hung
on the plaque that bears his name and loved hymns sung,
their hallowed words recalling once again
the blessings wrought by sacrifice and pain

as through unbroken years his church has stood
triumphant in her hope and brotherhood.

THE LINCOLN MEMORIAL

Although the sculptor's hand alone
could shape his visage and his bone
in a statue so revered by all
who daily crowd this marble hall,
eluding even sculptor's art
his timeless spirit moves the heart
as prophet's voice and poet's pen
bespeak compassion for all men.

And who will doubt when eager youth
on lonely summit stands for truth,
the vision shared, the young life spent
become his unknown monument.

LATE TRIBUTE

Those few attaining highest goals
rest in our Hall of Fame
with statue, plaque and lettered scroll
emblazoning each name.

The prophet jeered along the way,
martyrs who stood alone
for visions far beyond their day
now live in halls of stone.

THE FLOWERS APPEAR ON THE EARTH

Be gracious to the flower vendor who heralds the spring.
He stands on a slushy street in the cold wind, his cart
    overflowing
with rainbow colors that attract weary-winter passers-by.

A woman from a nearby store buys a pot of tulips for the bay
    window
of her dreary row house. A gardener takes stalks of pussy
    willow
and bluebells to plant in a corner of his yard. Young girls get
    daffodils
in fluted cups, and hyacinths are bought for sick friends.

In the din of traffic, the flower vendor, a simple man, longs for
spring and the solitude of deep woods, where carpets of
    anemone
and trailing arbutus are not for sale.

He parcels out daffodils and sells them for half price in late
    afternoon,
then counts his money and goes home, leaving bits of leaves
    and blossoms
scattered on the pavement.

He has had a good day. He knows that tucked in his rainbow
    cart
came the free gift of the first spring dreams.

FOR THE EARTH BRINGS FORTH FRUIT
BY ITSELF

After the storms and melting snows of March,
the violet appears.
The time of plowing and planting is at hand.
We cannot force the seed to grow nor hasten divine judgment.
For the earth brings forth fruit by itself and seed time
and harvest shall not cease.
God of the Seasons, whose power controls all Nature,
teach us to await patiently the fulfillment of Thy law.
Implant such ideas in our minds that we may reap the fruits
of the spirit.

HALF TONES

Buds are half tones in April harmony,
chromatic notes appear in every key
as choruses of yellow, blue and red
all sing together; mingled voices led

beneath baton of wind and rain and sun.
With half-grown buds arising one by one
as blossoms, full-toned, April goes her way
a moving cadence, leading into May.

AND ANSWER FOLLOWS QUESTIONING

Pale pink spirals appear in orchard rows, the elm
weaves soft traceries of green,
the tulip and bluebell spread Matisse-like tints
on greening lawns.
The pussy willow grows where every child may see.
The glory of Easter is all about us as April's pulsing
beauty dispels doubt and fear and lifts the wearied spirit.
Everywhere there is rebirth and renewal.

IN PRAISE OF APRIL 15th

Who would declare a single loss
when everywhere we see
the season's promises fulfilled
in bush and flowering tree?

Who counts deductions on a day
the flaunting daffodil
and spirals of forsythia
spill gold upon a hill?

And who can estimate the cost
of gifts received this year
or needs to count the violets
and stars as they appear?

PINK DOGWOOD

Pink dogwood in spring
so closely binds me to earth
I do not need stars,
nor any orb of heaven,
I am lost in clouds of dreams.

MAY COLLAGE

Trees that stand like dreaming brides
in white-veiled apple orchards,
Shaded lanes where pink dogwood lift star-like
blossoms high,
The flash of cardinals on the lawn and mockingbirds
that sing at dawn,
Women standing in open doors breathing the warm, spring
air,
Long twilights and the mist at night.
Light and shadow, color and shade, all painted by a
Master hand!

AS AT CANA

As spring slips into summer in the fullness of June,
so do our daughters and sons become mature women and men.
Bless them as they graduate from college and go into a
    competitive world,
far removed from sheltered campus.
Give them confidence and the ability to succeed.
May the newly married ones face their adjustments and
    problems
with forbearance and love, in honor preferring one another,
cheerfully accepting the necessary economies.
Especially help all parents who have lived for their children.
May they graciously renounce their initial claims on their
    children,
allowing them to make their own mistakes and never saying,
"I told you so."
This we ask in the name of Him who blessed the marriage at
    Cana.

COME AWAY BY YOURSELVES AND REST AWHILE

Summer at high tide,
Travelers crowd the highways, ships and planes
eager to escape the monotony of daily living.
They long for the ever-changing scenes: London at dawn,
Rome in summer light, Paris at night.
The provincial traveler is bewildered by foreign language,
exchange and customs officials,
The introvert forgets himself in kaleidoscopic scenes
and memorable sounds,
The religious worship in famed cathedrals,
The aged and weary rest by still waters.
Each traveler finds what he most desired and takes home
that knowledge he brought with him.
Everywhere joy and the wonder of discovery!

ONLY IN AUGUST

Half listening, now we can hear
the sounds of August, strangely sweet,
the steady whir of reapers' blades
slashing golden stalks of wheat.

Small choruses bewitch the night
as season of the harvest wanes,
While waiting by deserted shores
we hear the billow's minor strains.

When all too soon low humming sound
will end this August roundelay
only the wind can catch the sound
of longer night and shorter day.

THE FIELDS ARE WHITE WITH HARVEST

Day lilies touched by morning sun arise with golden trumpets
above low, whispered winds.
Tall corn stalks rustle on the prairies, stretching for endless
    miles.
Vines are laden with purple grapes,
Women gather ripe fruit and vegetables from lush gardens
on August afternoons.
The roadside is aglow with flaunting marigold,
The rising harvest moon bedims a golden world.
The season of the reaper is at hand.

HOLD FAST TO WHAT IS GOOD
AND LOVE ONE ANOTHER

September with crisp days, and the spice of autumn in the air.
Wine-red sumac and the maples turning gold,
A time of change and readjustment in our families,
when old ties are broken.
Our children go to college and we no longer share their
    experiences.
Colleges seem unfamiliar to us after the years. Our children
study subjects unknown in our time. They wear sloppy
    sweaters
and faded jeans to their classes. They are not afraid of the
    deans
as we were. They live in coed dorms.
We ask Thee, Lord, to keep them upright in their newly found
    freedom.
May they remember the things we tried to instill in them
    through the years.
We love them, but we know we cannot hold them.
Give us open minds and the willingness to accept their new
    world
as part of our own; let us not panic over change.
For we, too, must change and learn from them, as they grow
    into adults
and companions whom we both love and enjoy.

PRAYER FOR A YOUNG STUDENT

Reveal to his inquiring mind
the wonder of Thy truth,
let neither doubt nor arrogance
mar promise of his youth
and help him scale each unknown height
with deep humility,
assured new wisdom is but part
of vast eternity.

AUTUMN CADENZA

Elm leaves fill the air,
falling in swift cadenzas,
half tones of yellow, brown on brown,
repeated figures hurtling down,
diminishing in form and sound
till colors whisper on the ground.

AUTUMN ETUDE (AFTER STRAUSS)

As in Vienna wood
the scarlet maple weaves
a magic fairy ring
of interlacing leaves,
now darkening branches sway
to a Strauss-like melody
while children dance and play
in patterns one, two, three.

A TIME TO KEEP AND A TIME TO CAST AWAY

As one season differs from another in beauty, so do our years.
We are part of transition's mystery and slip from one age
into another as gently as autumn goes into late winter.
We are not dismayed by life's changing tapestries,
for in Thy providence, nothing is ever lost.
So guide us that each era of our lives means the beginning
of greater usefulness in another.
So often now the young are preferred today in business
and professions, but we should welcome them without
    bitterness.
Help us to find new opportunities as we grow older and give us
    faith
in ourselves and in Thee.
May our mature years be joyful ones and a crowning glory to
    Thee.

WITH GOLD AND SILVER

With amber grain and harvest moon
ripe pumpkin, clumps of marigold,
in yellow maples filtered sun
the autumn story is retold.

With overlay of beaded frost,
tiaras hung in cold, far heaven,
mute streams that lie in silver bands
are promises of winter given.

NOSTALGIA

On this isle life moves festively
amid tall coconut and pine,
a gentle tide stirs tranquil sea
and vivid allemanda vine
hangs golden trumpets on the wall
and here the heart may well forget
all save this beauty. No leaves fall;
these gardens will not fade. And yet

the dream of far-off closed-in hills
with whir of wild geese flying low,
pale asters when the north wind chills,
the spice of autumn, feel of snow,
lives in the heart that once has known
New England hills and now in vain
waits on this island shore alone
for one loved voice to call his name.

BE YE THANKFUL

How often we say "Thank you" without being truly grateful.
We accept blessings as our just due and our polite words and empty
phrases become devoid of meaning.
We are ungrateful to God when we do not consider helping others
no matter what sacrifices have been made in our behalf.
We take our freedom for granted and complain about our government,
and criticize our families while expecting them to overlook our own failures.
Dear Lord, we know in our better moments that gratitude in Thy sight
means service and sacrifice, not perfunctory prayers and polite phrases.
Grant us the humility to be truly grateful.

NOVEMBER TOPAZ

Now in November with fast falling leaves
the story of past seasons is retold,
red maple recalling wine reds of spring
while russet leaves are flying through the air
following paths the robin charted there.
Only the elm when torn by sudden leaves
lies pale and veined as a woman's hand grown old
where somber earth receives her offering.
November, a topaz in the fading sun
reflects all seasons, binding them in one.

NOVEMBER 22, 1963

Now that the golden sheaves lie dead
no fires leap from the mill,
dark houses hold their shutters tight,
the harbors hushed and still.

A sound of sobbing voices breaks
upon the silent air
with solemn beat of muffled drums
to cadences of prayer.

Now that the golden sheaves lie dead,
what of the ripened grain
and nations lifting futile prayers
mourning their leaders slain?

UNTO US A CHILD IS BORN

How beautiful is this season of the Christ Child's birth
with happy children, with homes ablaze with light
and cheer and solemn meditations of the Advent.
Because of God's greatest gift to us, we forget ourselves
in the joy of giving to others.
Winter comes with silvered feet, the brown fields glisten
and mountain peaks are softened with snow.
The season that brings the end of the year is the gateway
between time and eternity, for with each dying year there
    leaps
to life another spring.
It is a time when bells ring on the streets, carols chime from
    high
towers, family ties are more tender and we help the poor and
    unfortunate,
when we smile at the stranger beside us, and say "Merry
    Christmas."

FLIGHT

Though I have held against Time's reckoning
the memories and promises of spring,
seen summer harvest and the orchard rows,
stark branches bending under winter snows,
no season's glory I have loved or known
can match the hour when I must watch alone
earth's fading tapestries as last leaves die
and wild geese fly south in cold, gray sky.

PART III

This We Pray

MORNING WATCH

I keep a morning watch
and bring to Thee in prayer
small things that irritate
and those I cannot bear:
humiliation's smart,
the griefs that sear the soul,
and shatter those I love.
God heal, God make us whole.

WHEN WE PRAYED

We have not meant to be sanctimonious and demanding
in our prayers.
God, You know we are not saints: just troubled sinners
who want to be more Christlike.
Like Thy disciples, we would ask Thee how to pray.
Sometimes we do not know what to say, nor how to ask
for help.
Too often we use general terms like hope, faith and love,
when we should realize they are empty words if not applied
to daily living.
Help us to be vital and aware in expressing them and feeling
them in the very depths of our being.
We are so grateful to Thee, our Giver of life, for high
moments of joy, and for the depths of sorrow.
We thank Thee too for fleeting moments, fragile happiness
and
small annoyances, for they have taught us patience.
Dear God, we are not demanding or trying to change Thy
plans
for us.
Teach us Thy will and help us to understand.

THINGS OF GOOD REPORT

God of the Orderly Universe, keep us attuned to things
of good report.
Like Moses of old, we would see a holy flame in every wayside
bush and hear Thy voice above the clamor of the day.
Give us the serenity to receive divine revelation and to grow
in the experience and knowledge of goodness, truth and
  beauty,
with the faith that right will ultimately prevail.
Let us not repeat ugly gossip or be prophets of doom and
destruction.
With steadfast hearts, we will search for the truth and find a
mystic loveliness in all Thy children.

LORD, HERE AM I

As Moses saw the burning bush
and in His presence stood unshod,
now hushed before Him when He calls,
we too know He is God.
Creator of the Universe,
in all Thy world help us to find
new revelations of Thy truth
and share the thoughts of Thy great mind!

WHATSOEVER THINGS ARE JUST

Forgive our unkind judgments and lack of charity.
We are quick to condemn the actions of others without
knowing facts, setting ourselves up as perfectionists
beyond all law.
Our facile tongues provide panaceas for unfamiliar
problems. We glory in self-righteous pronouncements.
Unconsciously we contribute to injustice.
Only God knows what we would do ourselves if we too were
faced with problems beyond our control.
Let us keep a prayerful silence and not voice our
opinions, judging not lest we be judged.
And, in a moment of truth, ask ourselves and our God
if we could do any better.

ONCE SPOKEN

Think not your words are fleeting things
that veiled and soft as silken wings
will float upon the quiet air
and disappear—no one knows where.
For thoughts once spoken may again
awaken you to joy or pain.

Stronger than battles fancied won,
louder than vaunted deeds now done,
swifter than arrow ever sped,
they will return—the words you said.

WHATSOEVER THINGS ARE PURE

Lord, who looks on the hearts of Thy children, mercifully
save them from evil in a society that tolerates the unclean
and lets unbridled liberty corrupt all that is sacred.
Keep their hearts from evil and their tongues from speaking
guile not by law but by precept.
Living persistently in Thy presence, and in the presence
of the best of Thy abundant gifts, may their minds be filled
with beauty and honest purpose, shutting out all that is
unworthy and unclean.
Keep them always in Thy presence, not retreating from
prevailing evils, but expressing all that is good and true
in their speech and actions.
Only in Thee can they reconcile what they are with what
they would be and say, "To me, to live is Christ."

WHATSOEVER THINGS ARE GRACIOUS

Gracious God, who stands at the door and knocks,
forgive our impatience and the rude, inconsiderate
things we do in the name of efficiency and the desire to
get ahead.
Overlook our stinging, sarcastic words that are both
unnecessary and unkind.
We push and shove others standing in line.
We want the limelight for ourselves.
We ride roughshod over the inmost feelings of those
nearest and dearest to us, forgetting that the Master
Himself stands outside the door until bidden to enter.
We are inclined to overlook the gentle consideration and
courtesy which marked His earthly ministry.
Soften our insistent voices!
Love does not shout, and ecstasy is still.
It is not enough to be humane unless we are kind,
and pity without love.
God, make us gracious, make us kind.

IF THERE BE VIRTUE, IF THERE BE PRAISE

How often we consider our negative qualities to be virtues,
and boast of the things we do not do.
We know that if we think of things that are just, pure, of
good report and gracious, we will work to make them a reality
in ourselves and others.
Give us strong convictions and the courage to speak out
against all that is unjust, impure and ungracious, upholding
standards of conduct that will permeate the society in which
we live.
We want to be popular and sidestep moral issues like
injustice and racism, we tolerate filthy publications, we
are discourteous and rude if it suits our purpose.
Let us not merely be good, but good for something,
sharing Thy gentle, sacrificial ministry.

HOSPITAL ROOM

Along this corridor
in rooms with numbered door
and sterile white decor,
I see again
the human drama played,
hope as fear in masquerade,
the age-old cycle made
from birth to death through pain.

BE PATIENT IN TRIBULATION

Deliver us from self-pity that destroys us.
Give us the perspective to compare our troubles with
the tragedies which befall others more deserving than we.
Teach us to be thankful for our blessings.
As our Lord endured the ignominy of the cross, may we
accept our share of trouble in an imperfect world.
Forgive our emotional self-indulgence when we are
frustrated, and when we inflict our ugly needs upon
those around us.
Attune our unlovely natures in the loveliness and peace
of the spirit, where self-pity is lost in tender compassion.

OUT OF THE DEPTHS WE CRY TO THEE

Out of the depths we cry to Thee, helpless in our grief.
As Thy Son endured suffering, so may we accept the
misfortunes we cannot help:
when a loved one is stricken with disease,
when we are betrayed by a friend or are left penniless,
we leave it all to Thee, saying, "Thy will be done."
Guide each faltering step as we grope to find our way
back to Thee and to discover meaning and joy in the
things that remain: the dear ones who share our grief,
the majesty of a sunrise, the outstretched hand of
a friend.
So may we create beauty from the ashes of our dreams,
through trust in Thy protecting love.
Find some divine spark within us, that we shall be
more than conquerors through Thee.

THIS IS AMERICA

A desert sky of flaming light,
deep waterfall, foaming and white,
blue mountain shadowed by the night,
       This is America.

A mill town where the flames leap high,
white spires reaching for the sky,
blue ocean where the tall ships ply,
       This is America.

A humble school room on a hill,
White marble halls where men instill
truths for which they die at will,
       This is America.

Grim battle fields, where youth has bled,
white silent cities of the dead,
and all the pledges men have said,
       Forget not, America.

America, with flag unfurled,
where swords of hate and death are furled,
in a sad and war-torn world,
altars of faith with undying fire,
prayers for peace, the soul's desire,
love for mankind our hearts inspire,
       We are America.

THE PIONEERS

We remember before Thee the brave pioneers who lived,
not by sight alone, but by faith and insight.
They were the valiant minority whose devotion
benefited the majority.
They are now famous: the scientist who was ostracized
for his discoveries before they were accepted; the reformer
persecuted by the society he tried to redeem.
Bless those who would reform modern society; the old
and the young who are protesting against the established
order.
They condemn institutions, sometimes not realizing their
    value.
Give them mature judgment, and save them from hysteria
and destructiveness.
Teach them that progress is not advanced by unlawful
    methods.
Rather than condemning them, let us try to understand
    them
and, above their dissident voices, learn their real need.
May we never forget that our Lord and His followers
often stood on lonely mountains, apart from the world,
and protested the evils of their day.

LAKE TOWNS

They proudly flaunt broad avenues
and rows of stately, singing trees
that guard old houses, trees whose boughs
are vibrant with deep symphonies.
As hand in hand young lovers watch
the rising tides of mist and foam,
by lonely casements women wait
for distant ships now sailing home.

MILL TOWN

Mill town streets are long, dull lines
of company houses, dingy, gray,
and narrow soot-filled little yards
where unkempt children dance and play.

Children who see no sunlit days
nor quiet beauty of clear night
at dusk when mill fires sweep the skies
watch them burn in wild delight.

PRAIRIE TOWN

The low, flat houses stand aloof
on streets of storm-swept prairie towns;
defying wind and rain and sun,
they stay fast-rooted to the ground.

In prairie towns built far apart
with endless fields of corn between,
each man clings to the heritage
of Lincoln's faith and Sandburg's dream.

MINING TOWN

A winter storm is witches brew,
cold winds a winding sheet,
folding the last of fallen leaves
with mounds of snow and sleet.
An evil spirit drives the wind
galloping through the air
to crumble earth and flood the mines
till many perish there.

Grandmother sang an old Welsh song,
"Aberystwth," in off-key
then prayed her non-conformist God,
her Bible on her knee,
"The mine is dark, Lord, send Your light
to keep the lads from harm.
A pit lamp is but feeble spark
to guide them through this storm."

Grandmother prayed until the dawn,
certain at last that she
had foiled the witch and quelled the storm
with fervent piety.

LEST WE FORGET

Let us always remember the brave men who gave their lives
for our country and their bereaved families.
We pass Arlington cemetery on a crowded bus, weaving its
way through lines of traffic
Cars follow bumper-to-bumper, jets zoom overhead.
Everyone is intent on going home.
Dusk falls on the hills above us, veiling the white
crosses and gleaming monuments.
A beacon light shines from the Lee mansion.
A child sees it and wonders.
No one else speaks.
We are accustomed to the sights of Arlington: the Tomb
of the Unknown Soldier and the grassy slopes.
Any time of day we hear martial music, the echo of taps
and the final salute.
To some it is routine, but others remember their own sons
and relive the agony of the final rites.
They too are heroes, unknown and unsung.
Let us never forget their sacrifice.

SOLDIER IN A COUNTRY CHURCHYARD

(Stoke Poges)

He stands beside the time-worn bench of stone
on a narrow footpath by a brooding tree
in the country churchyard all the world has known
where once was penned the immortal elegy.

Untouched by time, the poet's grave remains
a humble plot where ancient ivies cling;
the elm and yew leaves hold soft-falling rain
and in the close the chapel bells still ring.

With sweet chimes echoing the poet's song,
the soldier wakens to this legacy:
that poems, not wars, can ease a nation's wrong.
Immortal words alone can make men free.

ARLINGTON SENTRY

(At the Tomb of the Unknown Soldier)

He guards this shrine with keen, unswerving eye
on silent hill removed from battles' roar
yet sees above him droning bombers soar
moving in formation to distant sky.

He longs to be where wailing sirens cry
and mighty towns are crushed to rise no more,
to know the moment men must live before
they leap from burning planes—perhaps to die.

He dreams of circling over war-torn earth
till dawn's bright spindle touches shrouded hills
and grassy slopes with flame. His proud heart thrills
that he guards those who died for freedom's worth
and for the nightly vigil, his to keep,
where unknown heroes lie in dreamless sleep.

CHRISTMAS 1970

Once angel voices in the sky
brought tidings of the Saviour's birth—
now deadly bombers fill the sky
and burning planes are brought to earth.

Once shepherds looking for a star
serenely walked Judean plain—
now on once-peaceful fields there lie
the broken bodies of the slain.

As Mary looking on her child
sensed cruel fate for her loved one,
how can I hear the Christmas chimes
when war and death await my son?

THE ROADS TO ARLINGTON

The roads that lead to Arlington
are traveled one by one,
where long lanes bend about the hills
each day processions come.
Passed the north gate opened wide
to a mound of upturned sod
that marks a hero's honored grave
to commit his soul to God.

All roads will lead to Arlington
from north, south, west and east
and grieving ones will yearn and pray
in vain for lasting peace
till from the bitterness of war
all mankind shall be free.
On calm Virginia hills will loom
a nation's Calvary.

HELP US TO LIVE WITH OURSELVES

God of compassion, help us to live with ourselves.
Day and night, we are torn by conflicting emotions
and problems of our own making.
Help us to be at peace with ourselves, that we may
be at peace with others.
Dispel false notions of our own importance as we see the folly
of taking ourselves too seriously, when there is
so much joy and laughter all around us.
Forgive the misery we cause by constant complaints,
intolerant attitudes, and inconsistencies.
We pray for world peace, yet have no inward tranquillity.
We protest national strife, yet quarrel with neighbors.
We mourn with the bereaved, yet at the same time we envy
a friend's good fortune.
Help us to put our cumbersome selves far from us,
and may our love for others transcend our desire
to be loved.

HELP US TO LIVE WITH OTHERS

We meet so many people every day!
Men, women and children crowd the streets, offices and
schools.
Many come unbidden to our door, interrupting our plans,
wasting our time.
There are happy and contented ones who brighten the day
and defeated people who mask their unhappiness with
arrogance.
We try to understand their needs: the irritable bus driver
whose wife is ill, and the overtired salesman.
Give us the grace to rejoice with those who succeed where
we have failed: the fellow office worker winning the
promotion we expected, the boy next door who received the
scholarship we coveted for our own son.
Save us from the misery of recounting our gifts to
others and expecting them to be returned.
Lord, help us to get along with other people.
Teach us that they too are Thy children, with the same
joys and disappointments we have known.

HELP US TO GET ALONG WITH OUR CHILDREN

Help us to get along with our children.
They are not ours, but Thine, and given to us for a
few short years.
We rejoice in their companionship and share their
happy anticipations.
Together, we appreciate the beauty of the world about us
and the priceless heritage we enjoy in all the arts.
Loving them, may we influence them by precepts,
not authority, never sacrificing moral principles for
expediency, nor insisting that they conform to customs of
a past generation.
They are but a loan to us.
We give them back to Thee praying they will do
greater things with their lives than we have done.

TWO PATHS

Let me walk on a path with tall trees
far removed from some peaceable shore,
on a road that is narrow and steep,
hearing winds and the billows wild roar.

Let me walk on the side of the street
where the humble folk live, and the poor
are aware of their pain and their needs.
Let me enter some shabby, closed door.

HERITAGE

Since to you, my children, I must deny
The heritage by which a man's wealth is told,
Rich treasures of land, rare silver and gold,
I have sought far finer gifts, that I
Bequeath to you for all eternity:
Songs that will echo through your joy and pain
And simple joys that you would live again
And solace find. The hallowed memory

Of firelight at dusk, that welcomed you home,
Tall birthday candles in their mellow light,
My swift reply when you called on me at night,
My love to sustain you, whatever may come,
That throughout all the coming years you may
Find the happiness that is yours today.

HONOR THY FATHER AND MOTHER

We are grateful for the days set apart to honor our
mothers and fathers.
Yet we are not content with the tribute we might give to
them on one day alone.
Though they would remind us of their limitations,
we remember their selfless love.
Father of mankind, may our daily lives reflect their
goodness and their teaching.
Keep us true to their convictions.
Give us a renewed sense of responsibility to coming
generations that the unspoken precepts of our fathers and
mothers will live on in our own children.

THE MOTHER

His mother followed all the way
that led Him to the cross.
She saw Him take the bitter cup
and drain it of its dross.
So, changeless still, a mother's love
glows through life's weary years.
And each, in his Gethsemane,
knows solace of her tears.

THE LOST GENERATION

They are with us in increasing numbers: the men who
have been retired because of age when at the height of
their abilities in business and in the professions.
A company executive is given inactive status on an
advisory board, the college president is eased out with
a meaningless honorary title, and the influential
minister becomes pastor emeritus.
The older and more infirm live in veterans' hospitals.
They spend their days telling of exploits at the Marne
and Guadalcanal, while playing pinochle with their friends.
Others, living with their families, spend sunny afternoons
sitting on park benches or playing with their grandchildren.
They read of elderly Congressmen and Associate Justices
of the Supreme Court, who pass laws and make decisions
which shape the destiny of their country.
They envy the man owning his own business and the farmer
to whom age is no barrier.
They try to contribute something of value to their
families and community.
God help them to feel that they are needed,
that they may recapture their sense of security.
They are loved and respected but they feel lost.

GOLDEN AGE

Old women, people set apart
in what is called their golden age,
can find no glitter when their needs
are great and pensions far too small.
Some use their wealth as a bright façade
to hide sharp edge of loneliness,
endowing symphonies and schools
or cruising to exotic shores.

In days of moon trips, they recall
when moons were part of dreams and love.
The touch of lips in country lanes
when horses sauntered the long way home.
Their bones brittle, their blood thinned,
each holds taut threads of memory,
while waiting, poised between two worlds,
and borne on tides they do not see.

ONE WORLD

At sunrise and at sunset,
the skies appear the same,
the sweep of burning candles,
small bands of yellow flame.
So the young and very old
live in the common glow
of understanding, faith and love
that they alone can know.

Theirs is a common language,
each being near the rim
of kindred worlds called life and death:
mysterious and dim.
The old, with wonder in their eyes,
find a heaven where they are,
and the young can catch the gleam
of farthest shining star.

EXCEPT YOU BECOME AS A LITTLE CHILD

Bless the generations far apart in age that love and
understand each other.
The young and the old, who alone are free.
They walk hand in hand on paths of unfailing delight.
They believe in fairies and angels with shimmering wings.
They share the same dreams and a sense of wonder.
The child finds beauty wherever he goes, the old
have learned that only love remains after the years.
They live apart from the feverish activities of the
middle generation and find magic everywhere.

HELP US WHEN WE CANNOT PRAY

There are times when there is no voice nor language
that can express our grief.
Give us the grace to desire Thee and to seek divine
guidance.
We do not know what things are good for us and are afraid
of making wrong decisions and false choices.
There is no straight path ahead.
We can only wait for the first glimpse of dawn after a
night of waiting, praying the numbness of shock will wear
off and we will be conscious of Thee and of those who care.
God help us, we are inarticulate before Thee.

JACOB'S LADDER

The slender morning glory,
deep rooted on the sod,
grows upward like a ladder
pointing the way to God.
And the dewy blossoms,
soft-hued with tendrils green,
are angel steps ascending,
each laden with a dream.

THE TRUTH SHALL MAKE YOU FREE

Let us see things as they really are.
We listen to clamoring voices.
We are agitated about the state of the world today and are
concerned for the future of our families.
We bemoan the seeming moral decline today and forget that
past generations have faced the same problems.
We forget the accomplishments that are our heritage.
That medical research has conquered dread diseases, and
educational progress has opened new worlds in science.
Our pessimism blinds us to the divine mysteries to be
discovered and revealed.
Help us to see ourselves and our families for what we are
and what we can become: our ambitions and limitations,
our divine possibilities and innate weaknesses.
Let us study to show ourselves approved of God.
Only Thy truth can make us free.

I AM WITH YOU ALWAYS

Each dreams his own dream of Eternity:
for perfect peace throughout the endless years,
for music that echoes through distant spheres,
and with songs of his immortality
breathes his hearts deep cry. But when I behold
each day some bright vision of happiness
and have joy that no language can express,
these eternal moments my days unfold:

when memory heals grief's darkest despair
in a child's simple faith and clinging hands,
in words unspoken that love understands
and faith like sweet incense rising in prayer
that throughout each dim tomorrow I may
find the joy and beauty I've known today.

IF THERE WERE NO DEATH

If there were no death, with its awesome finality and
incredible stillness!
If we never had to face the moment we thought we were
prepared to meet when a loved one dies:
We cry out in grief and bewilderment, but there is no answer.
We reach out for the warm hand that comforted us,
and find our world swept away.
Loving friends surround us with outpourings of sympathy,
but we do not hear their voices.
There are hushed footsteps and questionings, as each one
knowing death hears a whisper of his own.
For only God knows that the Valley of the Shadow is for
the living as well as the dead.
We walk there on uncharted paths alone, until a
    compassionate
and understanding God leads us through the valley to the
sunlit hills.
If there were no death, we should never know that, through
    Thy
grace, love can never lose its hold, and that neither
death nor life can separate us from Thee.

WE TOO SHALL LIVE!

Could life go out a singing tide
iridescent on a moving sea
or sun that fades at eventide
glowing in full majesty,
could all of Nature's forces here
but quicken when a soul takes flight,
winging its way to some far sphere
that is beyond our mortal sight.

But quietly another tide
comes bearing upon an unknown sea
the friends we loved who now abide
with us in hallowed memory.
And with what rapture they have gone,
their spirits singing toward the dawn
where loved voices they have known
will break the stillness of the morn!

THAT WHICH REMAINS

Lord, who in mercy sends
the sunshine after rain,
a calm wind after storms
and eases grief and pain
when we have suffered loss,
help us to rise again
to comfort and to serve
the dear ones who remain.

ACCORDING TO OUR GIFTS

May our ambitions be according to our abilities,
whatever our calling.
Temper our feverish desire for success at the cost of
integrity of character and personal relations.

Let us accept our unwelcome limitations and be willing to
sacrifice to develop our innate talents, never dissipating
our time and energy on lesser things.
May we remember always that the good is the enemy of the
    best.
We rejoice in the achievements of others and find harmony
and rhythm in all that is creative.
Give us the fine discernment to know both our limitations
and abilities and to make the most of our talents.
We leave the rest to Thee.

AS A MAN THINKETH, SO IS HE

Dear Lord, we have thought upon whatsoever things are
lovely, praying that we may reflect their beauty in
our daily living.
We cannot begin to comprehend all Thou has given to inspire
our minds and make each day a prayer and a poem.
We know only that something deep within us responds to the
cadence of language in Thy written word, the haunting lilt
of a Chopin waltz, the mellow, shadowed tints of a Manet
landscape.
After a summer storm, we see a wild rose and hear the
rush of bluebirds' wings.
Something echoes within our heart as we hear a child crying
or sense the agonies of a human heart.
We have seen defeated men and women rise to new heights
    and
overcome the world when everything seemed to be against
    them.
Dear Lord, refine us in a cleansing fire, if need be,
but keep us sensitive to whatsoever things are lovely!

A PRAYER FOR PEACE

Thou, who created distant stars,
whose wisdom guides the spheres,
grant peace throughout the entire world
in this and coming years.
For Thou, who marks the sparrow's fall,
will hear our humble prayer
that love unite us, heart to heart,
and calm transcend our care.

Creator of the universe,
such mysteries reveal
that we may use Thy precious gifts
to comfort and to heal
till everywhere, from sea to sea,
the threat of war shall cease,
and warring nations all shall know
the wonder of Thy peace.

YE TOO SHALL LIVE

With all of our assurances,
uncertain are the coming years
for those who have not learned by faith
His pathway charters all our spheres.
"For as I live, ye too shall live,"
He promised and we hear once more
His healing words assuring peace
transcending all the grief we bore.

PART IV

Think on These Things

THINK ON THESE THINGS

How wonderful are thoughts
that come on shimmering wing
of justice, loveliness
and every gracious thing.

That come from unseen realms
transcending all our care
and in their light we find
an answer to our prayer.

BE STILL AND KNOW

Dear God, who knows how hard it is for us to be still,
teach us the use of solitude and the wisdom of tranquillity.
In the din and confusion of our fragmented lives,
we know the world without and not the world within.
Help us to be still and to know Thou art God.
And, in knowing, may we discover the mystery and wonder
of the spiritual world
and find that silence has a meaning of its own.
In our tranquil moments inward voices will sing
the words of a lyric, the motif of a symphony,
and if we but listen, we can sense the longing in the hearts of
   other men.
From the kingdom within, help us to create a kingdom
   without
in Thy likeness.

KNOW THAT I AM GOD

All silence has a meaning of its own
far lovelier than song or spoken word;
there is new wisdom to be found alone
in solemn moments when no sound is heard.
In mystic language of tranquillity
love does not shout and ecstasy is still;
we deepen sense of our infinity
and far horizons we can reach at will.

LET ALL THINGS BE DONE IN LOVE

I Cor. 16:14

Blessed is the wife who is emotionally mature and not
    demanding,
whose sense of humor overlooks small annoyances.
Loving her husband, she does not coddle him
when he is moody and disagreeable,
She believes in him and brings out the best in his nature.
Her quiet influence helps him to grow to full stature
as a husband, father, and man among men.
Blessed be the husband who loves his wife and protects her;
who is not possessive and encourages her
to be someone in her own right.
He tenderly cares for her, shares her interests
and helps her to stand alone, if need be,
by sharing financial responsibility with her.
Blessed be the home where each member has consideration
for the personality of the other,
although they do not think alike.
Bless the family selfless in their love and devotion.

I HAVE CALLED YOU FRIENDS

In times of cynicism and changing loyalties, we often wonder
who are our friends, and whom can we trust.
Lord, give us confidence in the love and character of our
   friends.
May we never doubt their loyalty.
Teach us the laws of friendship in the surrender of our
   self-interest
for a genuine concern for others.
Let us not keep friends on probation but cultivate a sacred
   deepening
relationship through mutual self-revelation and answering
   trust.
We demand so much and give little, measuring our gifts
and expecting our grudging generosity to be returned.
We encroach on the privacy of others, knowing that,
in sacred respect for personality, each soul must be much
   alone.
Let us ask ourselves if we are good friends, dear God, and
   seek
to know Thee in continuing friendship and share Thy life of
   love.

THE GIFT

If I would make a special wish
for you, whom I hold dear,
it will not be the old, old one
for joy throughout the year
but that when darkening clouds shall loom
across your skies of blue,
God may grant you faith to see
the sunlight shining through.

And if you too would make a wish
for me just at this time,
may your art of seeing good
in other lives be mine.
Not to aspire for wealth and fame
but to the best be true,
for I keep wishing all the while
to be a friend like you.

IF WE HAVE NOT LOVE

Father of Mankind, thank You for our family.
We have had challenges and sacrifices far beyond
the wildest imaginings of the young lovers we were at the
    beginning.
Our characters have been forged through them
and the demands upon our patience, forbearance, and
our financial resources.
We are grateful too for the happy milestones: the high school
and college commencements heralded by school bands
and orchestras, playing *Pomp and Circumstance*;
the weddings with strains of *Lohengrin* echoing at the altar.

We no longer count the candles on birthdays, for we do not
    live
in years but in emotions' high days and holidays,
overflowing with love and laughter.
Morning, noon and nights repeat themselves in joyful songs.
For we have known heights and depths, birth and death,
parting and being close, and have been borne on the swift
    currents of life,
not measured by the years.
Father, we thank You.

THERE IS A TIME FOR ALL THINGS

Temper our love for our children with sound judgment.
Forgive us for overindulgence and our reluctance to
face the truth about them and ourselves,
for taking the line of least resistance with them,
overlooking their laziness and petulance.
Often they are not punished for lying and dishonesty.
We give them false ideas about themselves, knowing
they must face a world that will judge them
for what they are.
Our lives are not consistent with our teaching,
and we do not take time to share their interests.
Dear Lord, show us the way.

TWO WORLDS

You freely talk of outer space,
the distances between stars,
jet planes that fly at rapid rate,
the trip you plan to Mars.
I follow each imagined flight,
fantastic though it seems—
some part of me goes swift as light
with you in your wild dreams.

And yet your mind cannot conceive
my world, so paced and slow,
nor will your eager heart believe
what you will someday know:
that memory has bound me here
and caution stayed my feet.
Too soon their skeins will reach you, dear,
and then our worlds shall meet.

CYCLES

I will not raise my voice
nor am I horrified
when you denounce my world
in bitter diatribe.

Somehow your searching mind
has found a better way
to govern church and state—
I've let you have your say.

I wonder what you'd think
were you to ever know
I was a rebel too
a few short years ago.

BE YE KIND, ONE TO ANOTHER

Father of all mankind, bless our in-laws,
the family we joined at the marriage altar
in an aura of solemnity, soft music and roses.
Let us not forget they gave their lives for the
one we chose in marriage, and that our future
children will inherit their looks and traits of character.
We resolve that neither jealousy nor possessiveness
on our part will mar this sensitive relationship, so
fraught with tension as well as affection.
Guard our tongues should we become offended, and
let us overlook their foibles as they must overlook ours.
Give us courage to assume our own responsibilities,
expecting neither help nor praise, resolving all
possible differences in the light of Thy command,
"Be ye kind, one to another."

THERE I WILL BE ALSO

Be gracious, Lord, to all who pray
beneath the open sky
in coffeehouses and crowded streets
with friends and passers-by.

Without accepted ritual
or any formal creed,
they pray for all the suffering
and those who are in need.

Their simple words are guided by
the Christ of Galilee,
who healed and taught the multitude
beside a quiet sea.

DO WE KNOW HIM?

Bound fast by conventions
outmoded long ago,
slaves of wealth and comfort,
how can we hope to know
a Christ without status
the lowly Nazarene,
whose teachings changed the world
because a few believed?

ALL THINGS WORK TOGETHER FOR GOOD

May the Lord, who loved and understood both Martha
and Mary, bless all women who go about doing good.
Bless the work of their hands and their fertile minds
as they devise schemes for making money for worthy causes.
Encourage their willingness to study and become
informed on the problems of the day.
In their zeal for good works, may they persist in
constructive results, and not try to do too many things
at one time.
Working together in love and harmony, may the Marthas
and Marys avoid becoming overtired and irritable.
Let the leaders know when to retire from pre-eminence
and bring out the latent abilities of the
most humble among them.
Bless the husbands who stand by them in caring for their
children and who cheerfully eat TV dinners while
feverish activity is going on.

IN BETHANY

If long ago in Bethany
Martha had understood
the grudging services she gave
would bring no lasting good,
she would have honored Mary for
anointing with sweet oil
the Christ whose life had reconciled
dreamers with ones who toil.

THE BETTER PART

Take Meissen and old silverware,
the family portraits from the walls,
Grandfather's clock beside the stair
and costumes worn to many balls.

Take them, remembering the ones
who treasured heirlooms reverently
for generations coming on—
accept these gifts and set me free!

For I have found an April sky
beyond the tyranny of things,
above the clouds as eagles fly,
unfettered now, my spirit sings.

Nothing I own, however dear,
can longer hold me earth-bound here.

LORD, KEEP A WATCH

Once we listened for a baby's cry in the night,
startled by the first whimper.
Then came the years of sleepless nights, when our children
tossed and turned in feverish illness.
When they grew older, we looked forward to relaxation
and unbroken rest, but we did not know how soon outside
interests would claim them.
Now we lie awake until early morning, waiting for their
return from cross-country rides, dances and shows.
One by one they come in: we hear the approaching car
and give thanks that there were no accidents. Then,
the click of the key in the door and soft footfalls, as
they go to their rooms.
We recognize each step and can tell something of their needs:
weariness, boredom or exultation.
When the last one is in and locks the front door,
we relax, worn out with needless worry.
There are too few hours left for sleep.
We breathe a prayer of gratitude that once more
they are safe at home.

MOOD OF FRUSTRATION

So often we say, "Dear Lord, what is the use?
We have done our best and come short of our goals."
We are haunted by ghosts of fear and disillusionment
that stalk everywhere about us.
We know an executive in government who was dismissed
to make way for one beneath him in the interest
of government economy.
An artist playing difficult Scriabin
sonatas who receives critical reviews.
The efforts of Godly men to rear good families are a mockery.
Something dies in us, and, with our disillusioned
companions, we are in despair until Thou, Lord, reveal
Thy plan for us, and we learn that the race is not to the
    swift and
there is no short road to excellence.
Give us a long-term faith that sees beyond immediate results
and a vision not for today nor tomorrow but for eternity.

BROKEN THINGS

Gossamer dreams will return to you
out of the mist of your hopes and fears
quickening pulse, creating anew
fragments of beauty for coming years.
Dreams that weave poems from broken things,
fashion sweet lyres in hours of pain,
whisper as soft as the brush of wings
holding you fast in their silken skein.

DENIAL

Let me forget the things I sought for you,
safe islands where exotic fruit hangs high
above the common reach, meant just for those
who need not hear the rabble's bitter cry.

Halfway, you turned and found a sordid street
and squandered gifts I meant for you alone.
What can I offer now if we should meet:
I gave you bread that you received as stone.

AROUND THE CORNER

When around the corner from your door
you found a friend so dear,
you did not know such pleasant folks
were living quite so near.
When disappointment came to you,
and joy was turned to pain,
that someone cared just how you fared
made life seem glad again.

You looked upon a garden path
where the wild rose once grew.
In a lowly place, a pansy face
was peeping out at you.
You walked the street in loneliness
when nothing seemed worthwhile,
and were surprised when a child's glad eyes
looked into yours and smiled.

So you will find the things you seek
are often seeking you,
in the vale of fears and bitter tears,
there's a rainbow shining through.
Around the corner are bits of heaven
more real than stars beyond,
joys that await beside your gate
and friends you've never found.

THE LIGHTED SPIRE

The curving line of beauty flows
in rainbow arcs across the sky,
the contour of a Grecian urn,
crescendo note, sustained and high.

Within a given latitude,
the straight, hard line of duty moves
to undergird each lighted spire
and more than ancient theorem prove.

Uncertain lie the paths to art,
the fruits of fame are bittersweet
and few are they who reach the spires
where lines of toil and beauty meet.

HE IS WITH ME

Somehow I cannot think of Him
in some far-off place more fair
than this loved and familiar room—
I see Him everywhere
that beauty with her magic weaves
a golden filament
and where the ones we love have gone
on tender errands bent.

I see Him when the dull lane turns
into a cloistered place
and when on mean and narrow streets
one walks with God-like face.
Above the mingled harmonies
His gentle voice I hear;
abiding as the love He gave,
His presence lingers here.

REVELATION

All is hushed in the little wayside church:
no stately, soft-carpeted aisles run.
and past the narrow rows of wooden seats
no stately, soft carpeted aisles run.
No surpliced choirs there sing low, rhythmic chants,
no tall white candles on the altars gleam,
but on a rude table placed beside the Book
a dull, old lantern casts its flickering beam.

An obscure preacher reads the sacred Word
to humble people sitting just below,
so eager to know of the Living Christ
they sense his presence with a strange new glow,
see the dim room filled with holy light,
hear soft-sandled footsteps on the floor.

In white shining garments there He stands.
Lo! He is alive and evermore.